Cardinal

Also by Tyree Daye

River Hymns

Cardinal

Tyree Daye

Copper Canyon Press
Port Townsend, Washington

Cover art: Alison Saar, *Breach*, 2016. © Alison Saar. Courtesy of the artist.

Copper Canyon Press is in residence at Fort Worden State Park
in Port Townsend, Washington, under the auspices of Centrum.
Centrum is a gathering place for artists and creative thinkers from around the world,
students of all ages and backgrounds, and audiences seeking extraordinary cultural enrichment.

LIBRARY OF CONGRESS CATALOGING-IN-PUBLICATION DATA
Names: Daye, Tyree, author.
Title: Cardinal / Tyree Daye.
Description: Port Townsend, Washington : Copper Canyon Press, [2020] |
Summary: "A collection of poems by Tyree Daye"—Provided by publisher.
Identifiers: LCCN 2020017914 | ISBN 9781556595738 (paperback)
Subjects: GSAFD: Poetry.
Classification: LCC PS3604.A9884 C37 2020 | DDC 811/.6—dc23
LC record available at https://lccn.loc.gov/2020017914

98765432 FIRST PRINTING

COPPER CANYON PRESS
Post Office Box 271
Port Townsend, Washington 98368
www.coppercanyonpress.org

Acknowledgments

Gratitude to the following journals for publishing versions of poems appearing in this book:

Academy of American Poets Poem-a-Day: "Field Notes on Beginning"

The Arkansas International: "Ode to a Common Clothes Moth," "Ode to Small Towns"

Auburn Avenue: "Oceans on Either Side of Me"

Callaloo: "When I Left"

The Common: "How Do You Get to Harlem?," "The Motorcycle Queen"

Connotation Press: "Undreamed (Mother's Voice)"

Green Mountains Review: "Find Me," "Where She Planted Hydrangeas"

Lou Lit Review: "God's Work"

Muse/A Journal: "Miles and Miles above My Head""

Narrative: "By Land," "Ode to Sex," "The Shape of God"

Orion: "On Finding a Field"

Oxford American: "The World Grows"

Prairie Schooner: "Inheritance," "Which Ever Way," "Would You Miss Me?"

The Rumpus: "Field Notes on Leaving"

The Sewanee Review: "Miss Mary Mack Considers God," "Miss Mary Mack Introduces Her Wings"

underbelly: "I Don't Know What Happens to Fields"

Virginia Quarterly Review: "Carry Me," "From Which I Flew," "I Wanted to Place an Ocean"

wildness: "Green Thumbed"

I'm forever grateful to my teachers: Dorianne Laux, Joseph Millar, Eduardo C. Corral, Wilton Barnhardt, Belle Boggs, John Balaban, Rob Greene, and Vievee Francis.

Thank you to Cave Canem Foundation where this book was born, and to Berkshire Taconic Community Foundation and the Amy Clampitt Fund for giving me the time to dedicate to writing *Cardinal*.

Thank you to the following people without whom this book wouldn't exist: my loving wife, De Lissa Daye; my mother, Joyce Glover; and my family. And thank you to Gabrielle Calvocoressi, Bryce Emley, Sam Piccone, Leila Chatti, Nicole Sealey, Aracelis Girmay, Kwame Dawes, Rajiv Mohabir, Tyler Curth, Cortney Lamar Charleston, Clint Smith, Aaron Coleman, Karen Chase, and Emily Pulfer-Terino for your advice and kindness.

Dedicated to my wife and my mother and to the diaspora—

we are alive and everywhere.

There will be a day sometime in the near future

when this guide will not have to be published.

THE GREEN BOOK (1949)

Going where they'll welcome me for sure, oh baby

where the chilly wind, the chilly wind don't blow.

NINA SIMONE

Contents

Cardinal

Field Notes on Leaving

geography could not save me

Jacqueline Joan Johnson quoted by Isabel Wilkerson in *The Warmth of Other Suns*

*

the North Star is irrelevant

miles and miles above my head

I don't want constellations any nearer

I know there are whole cities all over this country

so bright you can't see the stars

the sky no wider than the heart is wide

*

the night President Obama was elected we danced
in the street of our small university
to *My President Is Black*   first time on my own
I was bright and felt like I had a father
                    every one of us was flying
a blunt passed around   we got lifted

my heart to lift

*

                        all the world to explore

if there were stars
                we could hold them

*

I've never been through airport security
without being pulled to the side and searched
to know you can die anywhere
doesn't feel like flying anywhere

*

I can't go to Canada
and leave my mama here alone

*

if you see me dancing a two-step
I'm sending a starless code
we're escaping everywhere

*

I can't afford to think like Whitman
that whomever I shall meet on the road I shall love
and whoever beholds me shall love me

*

doing the Dougie   trying to find the ocean
looking everywhere

By Land

I've lived on dirt roads that bent and ended
at a gate of pines,
the dust skipped up didn't make my mother
look like a dream. I've lived
on roads that dragged through America,
I've paced only them to the next town.

The road we kissed on is gone,
rich folks buying up all the city in which we make do.
I miss when Sonny could do a wheelie
all the way down Person Street
and no one would call the police
because he was a part of the neighborhood like the honeysuckle
bush between two yards, and he was beautiful,
not like a horse standing alone in a yellow field,
but like a man is beautiful.

Most of the little towns have a road nicknamed Devil's Turn,
where someone's brother died on a Saturday night
while Nina sang *Tell Me More and More and Then Some*
on the Caddy's radio,
the moon the color of the oldest cardinal.

Every road isn't a way out, some circle
back like wolves, you can't get lost on them
and they won't lose you, others wait
for you to run out of gas then come alive
with what your mother said would take you.

Every road promises something like a father does,
but when you arrive the town is empty, and you wait
like a child questioning everything, the road itself
laughing like a drunk man falling into a roadside ditch.

The road I'm walking now is howling and full of moon,
hopefully it'll lead to myself,
hopefully they'll take me home.

CopperCanyonPress.org

BUSINESS REPLY MAIL
FIRST-CLASS MAIL   PERMIT NO. 43   PORT TOWNSEND WA

POSTAGE WILL BE PAID BY ADDRESSEE

Copper Canyon Press
PO Box 271
Port Townsend, WA 98368-9931

What do you think?

BOOK TITLE: _____

COMMENTS: _____

_____

_____

OUR MISSION:

Poetry is vital to language and living. Copper Canyon Press publishes extraordinary poetry from around the world to engage the imaginations and intellects of readers.

Can we quote you? ☐ yes ☐ no

☐ Please send me a catalog full of poems and email news on forthcoming titles, readings, and poetry events.

☐ Please send me information on becoming a patron of Copper Canyon Press.

NAME: _____

ADDRESS: _____

CITY: _____ STATE: _____ ZIP: _____

EMAIL: _____

Thank you for your thoughts!

MAIL THIS CARD, SHARE YOUR COMMENTS ON FACEBOOK OR TWITTER, OR EMAIL POETRY@COPPERCANYONPRESS.ORG

㊟ Copper Canyon Press
A nonprofit publisher dedicated to poetry

Miss Mary Mack Introduces Her Wings

My name is   Miss Mary   Mack   Mack   Mack

       you sing it   my name

I turned into a bluebird last summer, I flew

through all the South. My wings are blue
and I touch the sky.

At first, I decided I was never coming back.

I took off my black

       housedress. I knew freedom

was not the act of flying,

       but the steady beat of wings.

It was my steady black,

       blue and my blues were gone,

I wanted to be

       a bird and became.

Where She Planted Hydrangeas

My grandmother migrated from South Carolina to North Carolina
with three children, a sister named Betty Lee,
and a best friend named Lue, they sailed here
and prayed God to line the highway with angels
whose wings could hide them from every evil thing
on moonless roads, the stars gone missing.

They arrived like most black folk looking
for more than a field to turn over,
to find a dead turkey vulture's feathers
scorched under the truthful dirt,
its wings bent as if it died
saluting the dead rabbit it stood over.

What stood over them was a field the hands
                    will never stop touching.

They slept on homemade beds and ate over fires
out of a cast-iron pot.
A whole community gathered together in the woods
to pull wild onions, to pick pecans
off the cold ground.

All her dreams she scattered
like chicken feed across the yard,
my mother, aunts, and uncles ate
those chickens and they sowed those dreams into us.
I purple under the windowsill of those lives.

The Mechanical Cotton Picker

for Black Chicago poets

It wasn't that they killed John Boy
        in front of his mama's small blue house,
and that no one called her Ms. Bluebird anymore

out of respect, though she never minded the name,
it made her believe she'd fly off some day,
or that the sheriff let John Boy's body sit
until even the babies stopped crying,
their eyes filled with him,
his body already going to marble
no one would be able to lift from their sleep.
It was that we could feed ourselves then
by getting down on our hands and knees to pick cotton,
and most knew what a body smelled like
blowing down a dirt road.

When Chicago reached my ear the war was full of bodies.
They sent whole train cars for us black folk.
I read the *Defender* and waited to hide my face
behind the curtains of a northbound train
and I prayed the train car would fly.
The South truly doesn't want us to go.

A Mississippi cop would catch a family disappearing
behind a rainstorm and send them home,
the clouds leaving four muddy fields at a time.
I left like a season's first lover across a window,

slowly like a southern sun
diagonal on a work-back.
I wanted to carry my aunts to Chicago with me
like this obituary-filled Bible,
these plums I got saved, purpling in my bag.

Ode to Small Towns

This where all the roadside memorials are,
        pink wreaths and dirty teddy bears.

This where a man walked when he wanted to fly.
This where he lay down and later died.
This where the train tracks folded the town in half.
This where that man who died loved a woman,
        that's his heart you hear, not the train.

This where I ran the dream-colored woods
and did not know why. This where I believe
a dog is buried. This where I danced
in the long moonlight of a field.
This where a woman planted ghost peppers.
This where she thinned her blood with root water.

This where you can see the whole town.

This where the moon never goes.
This where my grandmother hid some dreams.
This where my dead may have met.
This where they'll bury me.

This where I shot a bird from smoke-smelling sky.
This where it fluttered, fell.

I Wanted to Place an Ocean

I tell my uncle's ghost
don't waste your time haunting white folks who owe you money,

I try to give him my body but he won't take it
                            and pulls his wagon on.

I began in fields near pines where we laughed and fried fish.
                    If someone were to sing,

it would grow through each ghost

                    and be heard as geese crossing overhead.

The dead know
              the work they have done,

and if they are not careful their hands

will stay in the shape of that work.

My hands haven't touched cotton or tobacco,

I haven't pulled small green worms

or carried them inside with me hidden in the body's doublings.

I only was a child in harvested fields,

when my people let the cotton sleep there were no vacations,

the fields of Rolesville belong to my kinfolk, dead and alive,

and I don't know if my great-grandparents ever saw the ocean

                    or fell asleep on the beach.

Ode to Sex

Some nights my grandparents lay in a room
listening to their legs rub together
a sound like pulling squash from its vine
two bodies unraveling and rolling down a hill

Some nights they were so tired they lay there not moving
like flooded field-crickets
his hands still making tombstones
hours after leaving his job and the newly dead
Some nights she didn't care

if all the children still wandered around the house
she just wanted him to hold the moon in place
with his sliced
              and tattered hands

Oceans on Either Side of Me

Photo after photo measured our way

                             to Virginia Beach.

The family pressed against rest-stop walls,

on the hood of a car. We measured our way

by the fields connecting towns,

there's 23 from here to Raleigh, most of them tobacco

with big white flowers whose roots wrapped

around my grandmother's wings

                pulling a generation behind them.

We still know how to let our bodies go

to blooming. Now, a field measured out

and full of my kin.

Before I saw the ocean and took a picture of it on my phone,

I wanted to place an ocean in my mother's backyard.

I've always known it to be immeasurable.

Inheritance

My mother will leave me her mother's deep-black
cast-iron skillet someday,
                                   I will fry okra in it,
weigh my whole life on its black handle,
lift it up to feel a people in my hand.
I will cook dinner
for my mother on her rusting, bleached stove
with this oiled star.
My mother made her body crooked
all her life to afford this little wooden blue house.
I want her green thumbs

wound around a squash's neck

to be wound around my wrist

telling me to stay longer. O what she grew with the dust

dancing in blue hours. What will happen to her body

left in the ground, to the bodies in the street,

the uncles turned to ash on the fireplace mantels,

the cousins we've misplaced?

How many people make up this wound?

No one taught my mother how to bring us back to life,

so no one taught me.

O what we gather and O Lord

bless what we pass on.

To: All Poets
From: Northeastern North Carolina

It's just getting hot,
        dogwoods showering our shoulders with flowers.

I saw dead baby birds on a trail
  so I know new life has arrived

lost in the survival of pine and ash. I'll say it plainly—
we need you down here.

Yesterday, my uncle put a nail through his thumb
working for the same white man he's worked for since sixth grade.

Last night his blood fell on the bathroom floor and made a star
he couldn't follow.

He needs to hear your poems.

When I Left

a turkey vulture lifted from a field I still love.
It was hunting season, birds flew off
at the sound of rifles,
we warred with brown rabbits.

The vulture's head was bald and delicate
like the old men's in their hats
with names on them like Ford, USA, and Dodgers,

to cover their soft skin, old men
who stood in front of the breakfast truck stop
across from the field, the butter partly melted

in the middle of the grits, they also saw the vulture,
knew how to scavenge, gathered,
like horses or stars, in a junkyard looking
for a rusted pearl. Those old men have died
in their sleep by now, though no field could care
how many will fall down in it and why.

I want to sit here tonight still in love
and vultureless, listening to Sade.

I'm still the boy who walked through a dying
sweet-potato field, though our small town
wouldn't recognize me now.
I have a different body, a dented body,
fieldless and far gone.

Which Ever Way

I ran 95 north, 95 south, 40 west, 40 east
all the way to the plastic-filled Atlantic. I closed my eyes
to every rest stop, truck stop, state flower,
the broken heads of deer lining the road
like a parade crowd. Every tree on I-85 leans
over me like a holy woman, and if it could speak
would say again and again *the wind the wind,*
like an aunt after her stroke,
a mind on a freeway filled with unrecognizable bones.

I died on 96 north,
         I was a ghost on 96 south,
US 64 east all the way to my mother's house,
in every direction I was leaving, in every direction
it smelled like blood, a body under a vulture-filled sky,
a jar of coins my uncle kept on his dresser,
coins he hoped would save his life someday.

On the map I'm making, he's at every turn,
every street on the South Side is still black,
charcoal doesn't give you cancer,
so every night is a cookout marked by smoking stars.

A chalk-red cardinal
will always mean *I love you.*

The dead mark the living on bone maps
as whole cities they can enter
and walk around in with no reason to run.

How Do You Get to Harlem?

What did I know of skylines,

of a skin sea of brown faces not in a field

but walking down Lenox Avenue?

Our cousins from New York talked about Harlem

          the way our aunts with their Sunday stockings

over the shower curtain drying like tobacco leaves

talked about a heaven. I tried to imagine

a skyline where a patch of pines stood and sometimes swayed.

Every summer when they'd visit we'd make a moon around them

and listen to stories about city life,

my mother always in the background shaking her head—

she could hear us leaving already.

My favorite part was the train,

how it could take you

          where you needed to be.

Ode to the City

Because the trains in Harlem spill from the tunnels like butter beans

Because the snow in Chicago must be survived like cotton

Because in Los Angeles I flew

in my grandmother's blue housedress and Carolina wings

Because a skyline and a tree line both have a history of taking

                                      my sight and doing with it what they want

Because this block can't grow white tobacco flowers

to place in a window

Because a filled train car isn't my uncle's autumn-colored coffin

                                              with strangers at each end

Green Thumbed

for Aunt Margaret

my aunts type *amen* into comment sections

because they have seen God in even smaller gestures

whole kingdoms planted in their backyards

who knew a squash could say

       I love you

a river of water will not save

her husband's favorite tomatoes when she picks them

she tries not to think of his heart

they got their gardens

and a tree has never called them   nigger

God's Work

We dug a hole to plant the red maple

in memory of those faces and names we couldn't recover,

a tree of hearts if I look hard enough

and the shape of my great-great-great-grandmother's heart's

on our mind. The unnamed one

I want to name. I can't

even bring her to this poem now, a death that will

remain uncast and altarless. A hole

where a tree does not stand. A whole

people tortured in the name of God. I will save

all the blood from my mother's body as my testimony

to being here and alive, looking for a freedom

to place my black and ghosts.

Miss Mary Mack Considers God

No fence at most plantations. I still watch

what I sing, but I sing.

I think God must be a field full of caws.

I know God can't have a man's eyes
against a small body. There are no fences
because to run is to die, they must fly from here.

I think if God is a white man he sits low in his chair
and won't but only sometimes
make eye contact with the angels.

God is two black children sitting under an old oak
      that has not had blood wiped on its bark.
      Is a Sunday
      spent in the sky. Where tracks
      cannot be tracked.

The Motorcycle Queen

for Bessie Stringfield

You said you took God with you to all 48 states.

You caroled your grief on an Indian Scout,

rode your Harley until the crowd forgot it was a motorcycle,

saw a stallion riding the track wall,

breaking for a field's freedom.

You wanted a story you could tell

about surviving America on two wheels,

six years too early for the *Green Book*.

But I understand leaving.

I've been looking

to see the world.

The World Grows

Once, the world no bigger
than railroad-divided Youngsville.

Once, we made it to South Carolina,
all of us alive for the family reunion;

once, two miles from the city limits
my uncle was pulled out of the car
to have his coin-filled pockets searched.

Once, to see the ocean,
we took the back way out of town,

we lived in a circled path
and made do behind kerosene's heat.
Once, my mother in the shape of God

pointed to the moon in a screen door.
Around a card table with her brothers and sisters,
in gin they trusted the squash
would sprout a way.

Once, I trusted a hand pointing north;
once, I called for a wolf
and a man walked out of the night.

I walked Youngsville and marked myself down on a map
I was making.

Once, for my birthday,
my family gathered near the rusted cars in our backyard
in my happiness the color of balloons.

Would You Miss Me?

I'm far away from my living, the dead
in me are birds,

the wind finally gave my uncle wings.
I hope this storm miles off will carry me to him,
the heart is not a cardinal, it can't leave on its own
                                    without the body.

If wings grew out of my back
my heart couldn't take their beating, so I feed the birds
parts of me no one called beautiful,
            my father's moon of a nose.

I made a room of my grief.
When you ask to enter
                        it changes itself into a room half its size.

If I didn't return the way snowbirds return with snow,
songbirds return songs to one another across a harvested field,

the way my grandmother returns to my dreams begging me
to let her stay dead.

The light returning to her face in minutes.

Ode to a Common Clothes Moth

for De Lissa

In these days of less and less sun your love points and I follow

like the blind moths you beg me not to kill

half-asleep and the sun lesser than a minute before

I'll let you go into the night you say and I follow your love

of winged things to the back door

watch you empty your hands into the sky

In the morning you will wake before me

and walk out into the yard

the sun acts like a father as if it never left

moths sing of you from wherever

moths go to sing

Leave Yourself All Over

for Grandmother Carrie

Teach me to love
the way only the dead know.

Sometimes I want to see you so badly
I dream myself full of the reddest wings.

I do the things I promised my mother
I'd never do again.

You wouldn't recognize me now or the town.

Three highways
                    run through old tobacco land,

I weep all night for you,
will not stop no matter
the bright purple festivals,
the fireworks that scare everything from the sky.

On the way to visit your grave,
where you're buried beside your lonesome son
who walked Youngsville all day like an angel
no one would give proper wings,
I wanted to see you in that small town
where our last name watered a crop of soybeans,
labored under a white man's promise.

I wanted to see you in that wide graveyard as a cardinal.
When I arrived I wanted there to be jubilee,
chalk-red feathers darting the sky like a little blood moon.
I think I'll never be through with the dead.

My altar full of whole other worlds.
When you are no longer ghost
among your children, grandchildren,

when you become fully Angel, a bird
I let loose in my house,
will you still remember us and our jerry-rigged lives?

I know it's hard work being dead.

The Shape of God

I hold on to the shape of a star
the way my aunts hold on to Jesus's gown,
his whiteness they never trusted on anyone else.

I keep a star's shine in my eyes
behind the red they get after gin.
I stand under its shape,

I see like a bat
how the dead must see the living.
I made you a cardinal

because there're so many in this town,
and I'm tired of asking your photos to speak
the moment they were in.

My mother often dreams of you,
in these dreams she hates to hear you ask
what do you want, Anne?

A helpful dream, it reminds me to call just to say I miss the parchment
my mother made of her hands writing daily notes.
Reminders: *buy bread, visit*
grave, undream.

Find Me

It's been seven years and I haven't sent poems
to cover the gray stones.

You wouldn't be expecting them. I promised this to myself
on a night my mind swayed with ocean.

I heard the stones move like fish when you stare,
don't stare.

I prayed you'd pick up poems like Etheridge.

A tub of unshelled butter beans
on a dead woman's porch is our birthright,

if we do nothing else with them,
let's get buried in them

while they yellow, the sky strangled with useless stars.
Your first year gone,

I was saddled in my mother's Toyota,
we tracked a few miles to ghost-filled Rolesville

where the dead, where the dead was all anyone would say.

The apartment building in town is tan,
not bright red like it used to be,

all the stories are still death,
though they have changed clothes.

Today two blackbirds chase a crow
and I hope you're not running

out of memories. I hope now with wings
everything can come home.

Every bird in the kingdom touched our grief,
marked it as a country.

I ran ran ran to no blue ocean.
The color packs into me,

ivy grows behind my knees
in my mother's overgrown yard.

I Don't Know What Happens to Fields

I've never left this clay   I built a man with it
he walks around breathing and drying out

I've made whole days out of fields
I lay in as a child   the woods around them

have marked me with ticks behind my knees
scars like kisses by the smallest mouths
the train leaving Youngsville smells like my grandmother

walking into the open air of a dream
tracks all over America have bodies under them
still dreaming of mothers and babies

I found clay
in the softest spot of me   I pulled it off
I molded it into a splintered myth
rolled it down a hill generations long
so many thumbs pressed into me

From Which I Flew

Only together holding their hands in silence can I see what a field has done
to my mother, aunts, and uncles.

The land around my grandmother's
old tin roof has changed,
I doubt she'd recognize it from above.
How many blackbirds does it take
to lift a house? I'll bring my living,
you wake your dead.

We have nowhere to go, but we're leaving anyhow,
by many ways. When they ask   *why
you want to fly, Blackbird?* Say

I want to leave the South
because it killed the first man I loved
and so much more killing.
Say my son's name,

his death was the first thing to break me in
and fly me through town.

If grief has a body it wears his Dodgers cap
and still walks to the corner store to buy lottery tickets
and Budweiser 40s.

I don't like what I have to be here to be.

All the blackbirds with nowhere to go
keep leaving.

Undreamed (Mother's Voice)

undreamed my mother's tragedies
what escapes from the soles of feet in a soybean field

undreamed my father
       who in the end must've built his own tombstone

undreamed my son
buried beside my wingless brother

undreamed the South   giving me this tobacco
to grow alongside of
though I had to find my own water

a sun to darken my round face
           I can't hate a place

where my grandmother is buried
beside my other dead in rows

I want the dreams of birds
but not their eyes

their heads bowed as if sleep were a prayer
only the winged know

Miss Mary Mack Realizes Flying Is Just Running with Wings

I met most of the South

                without threat of a bullet or cage.

I was never a pet in a little girl's room.

A man in South Carolina grabbed me

        from a low branch but let go

        after I pecked and shrieked.

I remember him smiling as I flew away,

I thought he could see me.

A few boys chased me through a Texas neighborhood,

I was too blue for them to miss in a skinny pine,

their BB guns pumped to kill.

I hid in the big sky. Swooped and soared.

In those moments I felt back inside my-

self. Home. Human.

On Finding a Field

I've been looking for you so long

I need you so so

soso so   much   &

it snowed my woes

check my shoes   my purple hands

I've been looking for you   &

Can I plant my heart somewhere

in your mud? May I lie down awhile

under the magnolia in your middle?

Can I dig you up?

I've carried these grandmothers

and uncles for 28 years   my skin

wrapped stones   in my turning-over head

&

I need to put them down

Miles and Miles above My Head

my grandmother an unworkable field
full of shooting stars
in the soil of that field is everything this family needs
to turn our traumas into river current
for our children to gather our names
and cook a thousand birds to celebrate
My grandmother is a stone in my throat
my mouth full of old praying water
she died before I knew to remember her favorite sky
and I don't know the sound her tongue makes in the wind
I want to jar the soil under her feet in the last place she stood
I wish like I've never been disappointed
by the devotion the dead have for being dead
by how easily they appear and are gone
before the sky changes in April
my uncle died in his sleep   I was six
and had my grandmother's toes
sunken in wet sand under a waiting starless night
his death celestial   a death crowded with stars
Then I thought dying and sleeping were the same   both stood
on the same spot in my mind
the body new as stars once were
My grandfather built tombstones to sit on top of cooks
and maids they buried from here to Georgia
and he never hid his worker's hands
He spoke with bright white eyes
that my mother looked up into   watched him bloom
then wilt away   a squash vine's flower   a nova

Carry Me

after Langston Hughes

I followed the shimmer far down a road I still haven't found
the ending to. I picked up my life
my mother had sewn a map to the back of—
so one day I'd lay it out and travel back
to the flat land of eastern North Carolina.
A map to land where my body will die,
where my ghost won't ride the trains all night,
count steps from liberty to home.

I tried to find the ocean before I was covered in southern soil.

I put my head underneath the Atlantic, swallowed so many memories,

I'm filled with people,

                     someone has taught me to fly.

Whichever way I flew, my inheritance couldn't be lifted

from northeastern North Carolina's wet clay,

its hands hardened around my weighted ankles.

My mother's mother planted hydrangeas

where I wanted to place an ocean.

Where I wanted to place an ocean, she grew me.

I picked up my life for it was the only one I had to pick up,

how the body must pick itself up if no one is around
to offer a rounded hand out of the snow that only buries.
Stuck to my life were the same things
I carry back with me now,
my father's lying I've mastered and wear
the way a field wears the bones of birds.
The green tint of gin bottles my uncles made of their bare nights.

My mother,
    the only reason I have something to pick up.

Field Notes on Beginning

they each had a decision before them. In this, they were not unlike
anyone who ever longed to cross the Atlantic or the Rio Grande.

Isabel Wilkerson, *The Warmth of Other Suns*

<>

I wear my grandmother's wing-ready bones
                              like a blue unbuttoned housedress

through the city of festivals and fireworks that blow up in a one-cloud sky

Some nights the block tells me all its problems

The city becomes one mouth   its tongue pointed to the sky like a steeple

<>

I'll meet you at the hanging tree in Rolesville in 1957
I'll be the man in his father's hat
you be women back from the dead   we've decided
a long time ago the question is not how
can black people pray to Jesus? It's how can white people?
I'll meet you on a train headed to Queens
just tell me where   I promise to gather your bones

only for good   I was not touched by the darkness
between two buildings   I stayed in the moonlight

like you told your daughter to tell me
I don't want to die

in the South like so many of mine
I want to be carried back

<>

We were digging in a field you'd turned over
When you lifted the soil in your hands you knew its name

This is what you said was mercy ground
that I was safe here and I began digging again

I saw every lover who once held you
while your children slept
in rooms of so many blankets
one small fire for everyone

the blankets wrapped so tight
no cold could get in

<>

Leaving is necessary some say

There is a whole ocean between you and a home

you can't fix your tongue to speak

<>

Others do not want me no farther than the length of a small yard

They ask *where are you going, Tyree? Your mama here*

you've got stars in your eyes   a ship in your movement

<>

I said my few-note goodbyes   my dead will not come
I will not see a cardinal in the city

so I drew one on my chest
A coop inside a coop inside of me

Notes

"Field Notes on Leaving" borrows language from Edna St. Vincent Millay, Nina Simone, Walt Whitman, and George Moses Horton.

"Ode to Small Towns" borrows language from Larry Levis.

"When I Left" borrows language from Richard Siken.

"Green Thumbed" borrows a line from the documentary *Alice Walker: Beauty in Truth.*

"Leave Yourself All Over" borrows language from Rainer Maria Rilke and Aracelis Girmay.

"I Don't Know What Happens to Fields" is a line adapted from Larry Levis.

About the Author

Tyree Daye is a poet from Youngsville, North Carolina. His first poetry collection, *River Hymns*, won the 2017 APR/Honickman First Book Prize. Daye is a Cave Canem fellow and a 2017 Ruth Lilly and Dorothy Sargent Rosenberg Poetry Fellowship finalist. His work has been published in *Prairie Schooner,* the *New York Times,* and *Nashville Review.* He won the 2019 Palm Beach Poetry Festival Langston Hughes Fellowship and was a Diana and Simon Raab Writer-In-Residence at UC Santa Barbara and a Kate Tufts Discovery Award finalist in 2019. Most recently, Daye received a Whiting Award and the 2019 Ragan-Rubin Award.

Poetry is vital to language and living. Since 1972, Copper Canyon Press has published extraordinary poetry from around the world to engage the imaginations and intellects of readers, writers, booksellers, librarians, teachers, students, and donors.

WE ARE GRATEFUL FOR THE MAJOR SUPPORT PROVIDED BY:

THE PAUL G. ALLEN
FAMILY FOUNDATION

4
CULTURE

Anonymous
Jill Baker and Jeffrey Bishop
Anne and Geoffrey Barker
Donna and Matthew Bellew
Will Blythe
John Branch
Diana Broze
John R. Cahill
The Beatrice R. and Joseph A. Coleman Foundation Inc.
The Currie Family Fund
Laurie and Oskar Eustis
Austin Evans
Saramel Evans
Mimi Gardner Gates
Linda Fay Gerrard
Gull Industries Inc. on behalf of William True
The Trust of Warren A. Gummow
Carolyn and Robert Hedin
Bruce Kahn
Phil Kovacevich and Eric Wechsler

TO LEARN MORE ABOUT UNDERWRITING
COPPER CANYON PRESS TITLES,
PLEASE CALL 360-385-4925 EXT. 103

WE ARE GRATEFUL FOR THE MAJOR SUPPORT PROVIDED BY:

Lakeside Industries Inc. on behalf of Jeanne Marie Lee
Maureen Lee and Mark Busto
Peter Lewis and Johnna Turiano
Ellie Mathews and Carl Youngmann as The North Press
Larry Mawby and Lois Bahle
Hank and Liesel Meijer
Jack Nicholson
Gregg Orr
Petunia Charitable Fund and adviser Elizabeth Hebert
Gay Phinny
Suzanne Rapp and Mark Hamilton
Adam and Lynn Rauch
Emily and Dan Raymond
Jill and Bill Ruckelshaus
Cynthia Sears
Kim and Jeff Seely
Joan F. Woods
Barbara and Charles Wright
Caleb Young as C. Young Creative
The dedicated interns and faithful volunteers
of Copper Canyon Press

The Chinese character for poetry is made up of two parts:
"word" and "temple." It also serves as pressmark for
Copper Canyon Press.

The poems are set in Scala and Leviathan.

Book design and composition by Katy Homans.